Dressed for Success

I Talk You Talk Press

Copyright © 2019 I Talk You Talk Press

ISBN: 978-4-909733-43-6

www.italkyoutalk.com

info@italkyoutalk.com

All rights reserved. No part of this publication may be resold, reproduced, stored in retrieval system, copied in any form or by any means, electronic, mechanical, photocopying, recording or otherwise transmitted without the prior written permission from the publisher. You must not circulate this publication in any format, online or otherwise.

This is a work of fiction. Names, characters, businesses, organizations, products, places, events and incidents are either the products of the author's imagination or are used in a fictitious manner. We have no affiliation with any existing companies mentioned in this story. Any resemblance to actual persons, living or dead, existing stories or actual events is purely coincidental.

Although the author and publisher have made every effort to ensure that the contents of this book were correct at press time, the author and publisher do not assume and hereby disclaim any liability to any party for any loss, damage, or disruption caused by errors or omissions, whether such errors or omissions result from negligence, accident, or any other cause.

For more information, see the Copyright Notice on our website.

Image copyright: © undrey #196169638 Adobe Stock Standard License

CONTENTS

1. Carrie	1
2. The store accounts	3
3. A job is Seattle	5
4. Seattle	7
5. Carrie's first day at work	9
6. Carrie is surprised	13
7. Alice has a good idea	15
8. Where did you buy that jewellery?	17
9. Carrie's plan	20
10. Saturday night	22
11. Monday	25
12. Saturday	27
Thank You	29
About the Author	31

I Talk You Talk Press

1. CARRIE

Caroline Holland lives on a small farm in Oregon. Everyone calls her Carrie. It takes 15 minutes to drive to the nearest store. It's a general store. It sells food, farm clothes, boots, seeds, and buckets. Carrie knows the general store very well because she works there.

Ben Garden, who owns the store, is also the local postman and deliveryman. Carrie looks after the store when he's not there.

Carrie left school when she was 18 years old. She didn't know what job she wanted. She said, "I am not interested in anything. I am not good at anything."

Her father said, "Don't worry. You have the job at the store. You help in the house and on the farm. That's enough."

Carrie's mother did not agree. She wanted Carrie to have adventures. She wanted her daughter to have an interesting life.

Carrie's mother is deaf. She cannot hear. She was born deaf. Many deaf people learn to speak, but Carrie's mother grew up on a farm. There were no special schools for deaf people near the farm. She learnt to communicate using sign language, but she never learned to speak. Of course, Carrie and her father, Mike, can use sign language too.

Carrie's mother is an artist. She paints farmland, horses, and sunsets. She makes jewellery too. She uses stones, feathers, and wood. Carrie thinks her mother's necklaces and earrings and bracelets are beautiful. Ben Garden sells her paintings and jewellery in the store. Sometimes people buy them, but not very often.

Carrie doesn't know what she wants to do with her life, but she knows she wants to leave the farm and go somewhere new.

She dreams about doing something special. She loves magazines. She loves watching TV dramas about beautiful people. She likes travel programmes too.

Could I be a model? thinks Carrie.

She doesn't think so. She is very tall and very thin. She has long red-brown hair. Sometimes her eyes look green, and sometimes they look yellow-brown. She has long eyelashes.

But I am not beautiful. My nose is too big.

She has never had a boyfriend. She doesn't go anywhere, and everyone on the farms in the area is already married, or too old, or not interested in girls.

2. THE STORE ACCOUNTS

One day, about six months after Carrie started working in the store, Ben said, "Carrie?"

Carrie is counting eggs. "Yes?" she answers.

"Carrie, I'm having trouble with these accounts. The numbers don't make sense. Can you look at them?"

Counting eggs is boring, so Carrie says, "OK."

She sits down next to Ben. She looks at the rows of numbers. She can see the mistake.

"You added this up wrong." She points to a number.

Ben says, "I hate doing the accounts."

"Why don't you use a computer?" she asks Ben. "You have a computer. Why don't you use it for the accounts?"

"I bought the computer to do the accounts, but it's too difficult. I bought some books to teach myself, but I don't like it."

"I did some computer classes at school," says Carrie. "I thought they were easy."

"OK," says Ben. "Take the computer and the books home. Learn how to use it. Then you can do the accounts."

Carrie takes the computer and the books home with her. She teaches herself how to use the computer. She enjoys doing the accounts for the store.

I like this. I am good at this, thinks Carrie.

Carrie searches the Internet and finds an on-line course in accounting. It is not too expensive. She signs up for the course.

Now Carrie is very busy. She works in the store and she does the accounts for the store. She helps on the farm and in the house. She studies hard.

After six months, Carries finishes the course. She gets a certificate in the mail.

She takes the certificate into the store to show Ben.

"Wow!" says Ben. "Congratulations! You can get a job in a company now. You can look for a real job."

I could go to another place. I could leave here, thinks Carrie.

"Maybe it's a good idea if you look for a job," says Ben. "I am getting married. I am going to marry Melissa Briggs."

Carrie knows Melissa Briggs. She lives on a farm about 30 minutes by car from the store. Her husband died in a tractor accident, and Melissa lives with her parents. Carrie thinks Melissa and Ben will be very happy.

"When we are married, Melissa will come and work in the store with me."

Carrie is very happy for Ben. She is also happy and excited for herself.

3. A JOB IN SEATTLE

That night, Carrie talks to her parents. Her parents think it is a good idea for Carrie to look for a job in another place.

Carrie loves her parents. She knows it will be very difficult to leave them. She knows she will miss them. But she wants to try a different life.

She searches for jobs on the Internet. She sends letters to many companies. But no one is interested in her. She has no experience. She doesn't have a degree from a university. Carrie feels bad. She is also worried. Ben and Melissa will get married soon. There will be no job for Carrie at the store.

Then Carrie gets an email.

She has a job offer! It is to help with accounts at an advertising agency in Seattle! The salary is not very good, but Carrie will have enough money for a small apartment.

She is very excited.

Ben's sister lives in Seattle. She finds an apartment for Carrie. It is very small, but it is cheap, and Carrie can walk to work.

Carrie starts to worry about clothes. She wears jeans and T-shirts every day. In winter she wears boots, and in summer she wears sneakers.

She has some black high heels. She bought them to wear to the Prom in her senior year at high school, but she has no office clothes.

She finds an Internet site called 'Working Wardrobe'. It means 'clothes for work'. Everything is very cheap. She uses some of her savings to buy clothes for work. She orders two jackets, two pairs of pants, a skirt, and three shirts.

When the box of clothes arrives, Carrie shows them to her mother.

Her mother hates them. ---*They look cheap and ugly*--- she says with her hands. ---*The material is shiny. They will not fit you well. They will be too big for you.*---

Carrie remembers when she went to the Senior Prom.

Her mother wanted to make her a dress. Carrie knew her mother would make her a floaty, dreamy dress. But Carrie wanted a dress like everyone else. She went to Portland with some friends. She bought a bright red dress with a big bow at the back. It had thin straps. She bought cheap, fake gold earrings and a necklace to wear with it. Her mother hated the dress. She said ---*It is not a good colour for you and it doesn't fit you.*---

My mother is very special, thinks Carrie. *She has wonderful ideas and makes beautiful jewellery, but she is not like other people. I want to be like other people.*

---*I need office clothes,*--- Carrie signs to her mother. ---*I must look like a professional. They will be OK.*---

4. SEATTLE

Carrie is waiting at the bus stop with her parents. It is Saturday. She will take the bus to Seattle. She will start work at her new job on Monday.

Carrie is crying. Carrie's mother is crying. Carrie's father is laughing at them.

"Paulina," he says to his wife. "You wanted Carrie to have adventures. Now you don't want her to go!"

Carrie and her mother, Paulina, can't explain. Carrie wants to go to Seattle. Her mother wants her to go to Seattle. But they know they will miss each other very much.

Paulina gives Carrie a small box. *---It's a good luck present.---* she signs.

Carrie's father gives Carrie a present too. It is a laptop computer. "You can use Skype," he says. "You can 'talk' with your mother every day."

I love my father, thinks Carrie.

The bus arrives. Carrie hugs her parents and gets on the bus. It will take about three hours to get to Portland. Then Carrie will change buses. It will take about another three hours to get to Seattle.

The adventure has begun!

Ben's sister meets Carrie at the bus station. She drives Carrie to her new apartment and gives her the keys.

"Good luck!" she says, and drives away.

Carrie is very tired. She carries her bags up to her new apartment. She drinks some water and falls asleep on the sofa.

Carrie wakes up late on Sunday morning. She looks around the apartment. Her apartment has one big room, with a kitchen in the corner, and a bathroom. There is a sofa bed. There is a small table against the wall.

I can use it as a desk and a dining table, thinks Carrie.

She puts the computer on the table. *I must find out how to get Internet here,* she thinks. *I must email my father and say 'thank you' for the computer. I must email my mother. Maybe tomorrow, I can Skype with my mother.*

She walks to a convenience store and buys coffee, fruit juice, bread, yoghurt and milk. She makes breakfast. She puts the coffee and bread in a small cupboard in the kitchen area. She puts the fruit juice, yoghurt and milk in the refrigerator.

She unpacks her clothes. She hangs her work clothes in the closet.

She puts her jeans, shorts and T-shirts in drawers. *I can wear them on weekends,* she thinks.

She opens her mother's present. Her mother gave her a necklace, bracelet and earrings. They are beautiful. They have bird feathers, and wood and stones. They are very special.

Carrie cries. *My mother is wonderful. She makes beautiful things. But I can't wear these things here. I will wear black and grey suits. I have a white shirt, a grey shirt and a shirt with blue and white stripes. I can't wear this jewellery.*

Carrie hangs the earrings, necklace and bracelet on the wall behind the table. *I can think about my mother every time I look at these beautiful things,* she thinks.

5. CARRIE'S FIRST DAY AT WORK

Carrie does not sleep well. She is excited about her first day at her new job. She is nervous too. She wakes up early. She makes breakfast. She puts on one of her suits with a grey shirt.

She walks to the building where Fraser and Slater Advertising have their offices.

She looks at the board in the entrance lobby. Fraser and Salter are on the 5th floor.

She waits at the elevator. A man in a formal business suit comes into the building. He stands next to her.

The elevator door opens. Carrie walks into the elevator. The man follows her.

"Eighth floor?" he asks.

"No," says Carrie. "Fifth floor."

The man looks at her. "The law firm is on the eighth floor," he says.

Carrie thinks he is strange. "I want Fraser and Slater Advertising," she says.

"OK, sorry," says the man.

The elevator stops at the 5th floor and Carrie walks to the big glass doors of Fraser and Slater Advertising. The door is locked. There is no one there.

Carrie looks at the clock on the wall. It is 8:00am. Carrie waits. She waits for a long time. At 8:45am, the elevator stops on the 5th floor, and a young woman gets out.

She takes a key card from her bag and opens the door.

"Can I help you?" she says to Carrie.

"I'm Carrie Holland. I am starting work here today."

The young woman is surprised. "Oh. I didn't know. Who are you going to be working with?"

"I got an email letter from Bella Overton. I'm going to be helping with the accounts."

"Come in and wait," says the young woman. "I'm Alice Baxter. I work on the front desk here. No one else ever comes in before nine o'clock or even nine thirty."

Carrie sits on a sofa in the reception area and waits. Alice is sitting at her desk. Carrie is very interested in Alice.

Alice is short. She has black and blue curly hair. Her eyes are black and very bright. She is wearing silver ankle boots and short black pants. Her T-shirt is bright pink and has silver spots on it.

They are strange clothes to wear to work, thinks Carrie. *I wonder why she is wearing those clothes?*

Alice is painting her fingernails silver. She waves her hands at Carrie.

"Do you want to make us a cup of coffee? There's a little kitchen behind my desk."

Carrie makes coffee and gives a cup to Alice.

The phone rings, and Carrie goes back to sit on the sofa. At about 9:15am, people start arriving for work.

They are wearing boots, jeans, sweatshirts, casual shirts and denim jackets. No one is wearing a suit.

My clothes are wrong, thinks Carrie. *But I have no money to buy new ones.*

Finally, at 10:00am, a woman dressed in black comes into the office.

"Bella," says Alice. "Your accounts assistant is waiting for you."

The woman talks to Carrie. "I'm Bella Overton," she says.

This is my new boss, thinks Carrie.

"Thank you for hiring me," says Carrie. "I will work very hard for you."

Bella says, "Come with me."

She takes Carrie to a large room full of people. They are talking and laughing. There are whiteboards and computers everywhere. In one corner is a small desk.

"This is your desk," says Bella. "My office is over there."

Carrie sees a row of offices along one side of the room. Bella is pointing to an office at the far end of the room.

"Thank you," says Carrie. "What do you want me to do?"

"I don't know," says Bella. "I must give you something to do. Wait here."

Carrie stands next to the small, empty desk and waits. Bella comes back with a box of paper.

"Put these papers through the paper shredder," she says, and she walks away.

Carrie goes out to talk to Alice.

"Where is the paper shredder?" she asks. "Bella gave me some papers to shred."

Alice smiles at Carrie. "She didn't tell you?"

"No," says Carrie.

"I'm sorry," says Alice. "Bella is not very nice. I don't like her."

Bella is my new boss, thinks Carrie. I can't say anything.

Alice tells Carrie the paper shredder is in the photocopying room.

Carrie takes the box of papers and starts the shredding machine. She looks at all the papers before she shreds them. They are copies of accounts.

I want to be good at my job, she thinks. *This will be a good way to learn.*

It is a strange day. When Carrie finishes the box of papers, she goes to Bella's office. Bella is talking on the telephone. When Bella stops talking, Carrie knocks on the door.

"What shall I do now?" she asks.

"I'm busy," says Bella. "Go and have lunch. Don't come back until two o'clock."

It's only twelve o'clock! thinks Carrie.

"Yes, Bella," she says.

Carrie buys a sandwich and a can of coke from a convenience store. She sits in a park to eat her lunch. Then she waits until it is time to go back to the office. She sits at her desk and waits. It is a long and boring afternoon.

At 6:00pm, Alice comes to Carrie's desk.

"Go home," she says. "Bella won't come back now."

Carrie goes home. She makes a turkey sandwich. She sends an email to her mother. Her mother turns on Skype. Carrie is very pleased to see her mother.

---*How was your first day?*--- asks her mother.

---*It was great.*--- Carries tells her mother. She does not tell her mother her work clothes are wrong. She does not tell her mother she does not like her boss. ---*My job is wonderful!*---

6. CARRIE IS SURPRISED

Every day, Carrie arrives at work at 9:00am. She makes coffee. If Alice is not busy, they talk.

Carrie likes Alice very much. On Tuesday and Wednesday, Alice and Carrie eat lunch together.

She waits for Bella to come to work. Bella comes to work late. She gives Carrie some work to do. She tells her to file papers. She tells her to make labels for boxes. She tells her to make coffee, or to go and buy cookies or sandwiches. Carrie is not happy. "I want to do accounts work. I don't want to be an office girl," she says to Alice.

Alice laughs. "You do not have a nice boss, but you have a job. You are living in Seattle. It is a great city!"

On Thursday, Alice says, "I have news for you. Tomorrow there will be a client party. It will be in a big hotel. We will all go to the party."

"All of us?"

"Yes. We will all go to the party. It will be fun!"

Bella gives Carrie another box of papers for the shredder. Carrie is thinking about the party, but she is also reading the papers before she puts them in the shredding machine.

Something is very strange, thinks Carrie. *These look like the same papers I put through the shredding machine on Monday. But the numbers are different.*

Carrie has a good memory. She thinks she has seen these papers before. The clients are the same, the dates are the same, but the numbers are different.

Carrie goes to talk to Alice.

"Is Bella the boss of this company?" asks Carrie.

Alice laughs. "No! She is the accounts person. Mr Slater and Mr Fraser own the company. Mr Fraser is retired now, so the boss is Mr Slater. He is away playing golf, but he will be back for the party."

Then Alice looks serious. "What are you going to wear to the party?"

"It's a work party," says Carrie. "I'll wear the same clothes I wear to work."

"No!" says Alice. "I really like you, Carrie. But I hate your clothes. You can't wear one of your work suits to the party. Fraser and Slater's clients are in the fashion industry. There will be models at the party. There will be people from fashion magazines. They will all be wearing stylish clothes. Tomorrow at lunchtime, we'll go shopping."

"I can't," says Carrie sadly. "The company hasn't paid me yet, and I don't have any money. I guess I won't go to the party."

"Of course you will go to the party!" says Alice. "I can't lend you my clothes. They will be too small for you. But I have an idea. The party starts at seven thirty. Tomorrow we will leave work early. We will go to your apartment. I will do your hair, and I will find you something to wear!"

7. ALICE HAS A GOOD IDEA

Alice and Carrie leave work a little early, and walk to Carrie's apartment. Today Alice is wearing red basketball shoes, a long skirt with orange and purple flowers, and a pale blue cardigan. Alice will not wear these clothes to the party. Alice has a bag with her clothes for the party.

Alice pulls Carrie's clothes out of the closet and the drawers. She throws them on the sofa.

"Let me think," she says.

"I'm hungry," says Carrie. "Would you like a peanut butter sandwich?"

"Yes, please," says Alice.

Carrie makes the sandwiches and fills glasses with milk. She takes them to the little table.

Alice is picking up clothes and throwing them down. She is talking to herself.

"No ideas! What can Carrie wear to the party?"

"Come and eat something!" says Carrie, laughing.

Alice sits down at the little table and looks at the wall. She sees the earrings, necklace and bracelet made from wood, feathers and stones. It is the jewellery Carrie's mother made for her.

"That's it!" shouts Alice. "I know what you will wear to the party!"

Alice eats her sandwich quickly. "Do you have scissors?"

Carrie gives Alice a pair of scissors. Alice takes a pair of old jeans from the sofa and cuts the bottom off the legs.

When Carrie is dressed, she is wearing the old jeans. They are cut off to just below her knees. She is wearing Alice's pale blue cardigan. Alice is much smaller than Carrie, so the cardigan is short and tight. She is wearing high-heeled cowboy boots.

"Sit down," says Alice. "I will do your hair." Alice is very quick. She makes a lot of small braids in the top of Carrie's hair. The rest of Carrie's hair falls loose down her back.

Alice takes the necklace and earrings from the wall and gives them to Carrie. "Put these on," she says. "I must get dressed."

When Carrie looks in the mirror, she is very surprised.

Alice is clever, she thinks. *I look very different.*

Alice dresses quickly and puts on some make up. Carrie looks at her.

"Wow," she says. "You look great!"

Alice is wearing a man's tuxedo jacket as a dress. She is wearing her short silver boots and a man's hat. Her lipstick is very bright red.

"You look good too," says Alice. "You must wear clothes like this to work. Put your business suits in the garbage!"

8. WHERE DID YOU BUY THAT JEWELLERY?

Carrie is enjoying the party, but she feels shy because there are many stylish people there. Some of the people from the office are very kind. They come and talk to her. They say, "You look great!"

Carrie says, "Thank Alice! These clothes were her idea."

Bella is there. She is wearing a black lace dress. She doesn't talk to Carrie.

Carrie is happy to stand near a wall and watch everyone. She loves fashion magazines and she sees a famous model.

I saw her picture in a fashion magazine! This party is exciting.

"Excuse me!" A woman is talking to Carrie.

Carrie is surprised.

"Sorry," she says.

"Excuse me," says the woman. She has very short white hair. She is wearing a bright green dress. "Where did you buy that necklace and earrings?"

"I didn't buy them," says Carrie. "My mother made them for me."

"Your mother?"

"Yes."

"I want them for a photo shoot," says the woman. "I will buy them for one thousand five hundred dollars."

"One thousand five hundred dollars!" Carrie is very surprised. Then she thinks, *My mother made these for me. I can't sell them.*

"I'm sorry. I can't sell them. They were a present."

"OK," says the woman. "If you lend them to me for the photo shoot, I will give you one thousand five hundred dollars. Do you have any more jewellery like this?"

When Ben puts my mother's jewellery in his store, he sells it for ten or fifteen dollars! thinks Carrie.

"Yes," says Carrie. "I have some more in my apartment. And my mother has much more jewellery at home."

"This is good," says the woman. "What magazine do you work for?"

"Uh. I work for Fraser and Slater. I work in the office."

The woman laughs. "You don't look like an office worker!"

"Usually, I look like an office worker. My friend, Alice, chose this outfit for me."

"Is your friend here?" asks the woman.

Carrie looks around the room. "She is standing by the bar. She is the one in the man's hat."

"Oh," says the woman. "I saw her before. She has good style. Here is my card." The woman gives Carrie a business card. Carrie reads it.

--- *Alexa Hobermeyer, Fashion Features Coordinator 'Glitzy'.* ---

"*Glitzy!*" says Carrie. "I love your magazine."

"That's good," says Alexa. "Give me your address. Tomorrow morning at five o'clock, someone will come to your house. Give them all the jewellery from your mother. I will pay you to lend it to me."

Alexa walks away, but then she comes back. "What is the name of the maker? We will put it in the magazine."

"Paulina," says Carrie.

"OK," says Alexa. "'Jewellery by Paulina'. When the fashion feature is in *Glitzy*, everyone will want to buy jewellery made by Paulina."

Carrie feels very tired. She wants to go home. She finds Alice and says, "I'm going home now."

"I want to party!" says Alice. "My work clothes are at your apartment. Can I come tomorrow to get my clothes?"

"Yes," says Carrie. "I talked to Alexa Hobermeyer. I want to tell you what she said."

"Alexa Hobermeyer!" Alice is excited. "What did she say?"

"Tomorrow," says Carrie. "I will tell you tomorrow."

Carrie Skypes her mother before she goes to bed. Her mother signs ---*I like your hair. It looks good. Did you enjoy the party?*---

---Yes.--- signs Carry.

---You are wearing your good luck jewellery. I'm happy. I'm pleased you like it.---

---I love it and some people were very interested in it.---

Carrie does not tell her mother about Alexa Hobermeyer. *I will wait until Alexa gives me the money. I will give the money to my mother. It will be a great surprise for her. I hope they use the jewellery in the photo shoot. My mother will see her work in Glitzy! That will be exciting for her.*

Carrie takes off the jewellery.

Maybe my mother can sell more of her jewellery. Maybe there are people who like jewellery made from stones and feathers.

Carrie goes to sleep but she doesn't dream about fashion magazines or jewellery.

She dreams about numbers.

9. CARRIE'S PLAN

On Saturday morning Carrie wakes up very early. She puts all her mother's jewellery in a box.

At 5:00am, a courier comes to Carrie's apartment and takes the box away.

Carrie sits for a long time thinking about the papers she put through the shredding machine.

Something is wrong. I know it. Bella didn't give me a computer. She doesn't want me to look at the accounts. I want to know more about these accounts.

Carrie makes a plan.

Alice comes to Carrie's apartment. They drink sodas, and talk about the party. Carrie tells Alice about Alexa Hobermeyer and the jewellery.

Alice thinks it is a wonderful chance for Carrie's mother.

Carrie tells Alice that Alexa Hobermeyer said 'Alice has good style'.

Alice is very pleased.

Carrie makes omelettes and salad for lunch.

Then she says to Alice, "I want to talk to you about something else."

"Bella gave me papers to shred. But something is wrong," says Carrie. "Bella gave me a job to help with the accounts. But I have no computer at work. Bella does not ask me to help with the accounts. I think she doesn't want me to see them. I want to look at Bella's computer, but I need your help."

Alice is very interested. "How can I help you?"

"You have a key card to open the front door to the office. Will your key card open Bella's office door too?"

"Yes. My key card opens all the doors in Fraser and Slater's offices. And I know how to turn off the security system too. I do it every morning because I am the first person to come to work."

"I want to go to the offices tonight. Will you lend me your card?"

"No," says Alice. "I won't lend you my card because I am going to come with you!"

Alice looks at Carrie's laptop. "Can you copy the files onto a memory stick and bring them back here?"

"No," says Carrie. "I don't have the right software. I will have to do everything in Bella's office. I want to find out what is happening. But I don't want you to be in trouble."

"I don't care," says Alice. "I don't like Bella and I think you are right. There is something wrong with the accounts. If I am in trouble and I lose my job, I will go and talk to Alexa Hobermeyer. She said, 'I have good style!' Maybe she will give me a job!"

10. SATURDAY NIGHT

Carrie and Alice go to the office building on Saturday night. Alice uses her key card to open the front door of Fraser and Slater Advertising. She turns off the security system.

They do not turn any lights on. The lights from the street are bright enough to see the way to Bella's office.

Alice opens the door to Bella's office. Carrie sits down at the desk and turns on Bella's computer.

"Oh no!" she says. "I don't know the password! I can't look at anything!"

Alice laughs. "I think I can guess Bella's password," she says. "Try 'beautiful'!"

Carrie types in 'beautiful'. "No, it doesn't work," she says.

Alice thinks. "Try 'Number1'."

Carrie types in 'Number1'. It is not the right password. Then she tries '#1beautiful'.

"Yes!" she shouts. "I'm in! You are very clever, Alice."

Carrie starts opening files and checking the company accounts. She makes a spreadsheet. It takes a long time.

Alice is bored. She lies down on the floor behind the desk, and goes to sleep.

Finally, Carrie knows everything.

I know what Bella is doing. We must tell Mr Slater.

Just then, Bella comes to the door of the office. She is very angry.

"What are you doing here?" she shouts.

Carrie says, "I shredded the papers you gave me. Sometimes the papers were the same. I knew something was wrong. I came to look at your computer. Now I know what is wrong.

"You are stealing money from this company. You make two accounts for every job. One is for more money. You show Mr Slater one account, but you send an account for more money to the client. You are keeping the extra money."

"Yes," says Bella. "It is very easy, and I like money. But I had a problem."

"Alexa Hobermeyer asked Mr Slater about an account I sent to *Glitzy* magazine. She said it was too much money. Mr Slater agreed. He was very angry. I told him I made a mistake. I said I was tired. I had too much work to do. He told me to hire someone to help me. I chose you."

Why did you choose me?" asks Carrie.

"You have no experience," says Bella. "You only have a certificate from a distance learning school. I thought you are too young, and too stupid to understand what I am doing. But I was wrong. So, you are going to die."

Bella takes a gun from her handbag.

"Open the window," says Bella. "You will jump out the window and you will die. I will tell everyone the job was too difficult for you."

"No!" shouts Carrie.

Carrie is standing behind the desk. Bella walks towards Carrie and puts the gun against Carrie's neck. She holds Carrie's arm tightly.

Alice is lying on the floor. She is very shocked and very frightened, but she wants to help Carrie. *Bella doesn't know I am here,* thinks Alice. What can I do?

"Now!" shouts Bella. "Go to the window!"

Carrie moves towards the window.

Alice jumps at Bella's knees. Bella drops the gun. Bella falls down. She hits her head on the corner of the desk. She falls down on the floor. Alice jumps on Bella's back.

Bella is kicking. She is trying to attack Alice, but Alice is lying on Bella's back.

"Call the police! Quickly!" shouts Alice. "I can't hold her."

Carrie dials 911.

The police come very quickly. The police take Bella to the hospital. Carrie and Alice answer many questions.

Alice calls Mr Slater. He comes to the office. Carrie and Alice answer more questions. They are both very tired.

Mr Slater is very surprised by Carrie's story.

"I did not know anything," he says. "I think you are very clever. It was a lucky day when you came to work here."

It is 3:00am before Carrie and Alice can go home.

Carrie sleeps most of Sunday.

11. MONDAY

On Monday morning, Carrie goes to work early. Alice and Carrie talk about Saturday night.

"We were so lucky that Bella didn't see you," Carrie says to Alice. "You saved my life!"

"I was very scared," says Alice. "I didn't like Bella, but I didn't think she was such a dangerous person."

Mr Slater calls Carrie and Alice to his office. "You are very brave women," he says. "You will be our new accounts person," he says to Carrie. "I will pay you a lot more money, and we will find someone to help you."

Carrie is happy.

"What can I do for you?" Mr Slater asks Alice.

"Mmm. I don't want to work here anymore," says Alice. "Will you help me get a job with a fashion magazine?"

"Of course! Yes!" says Mr Slater.

Mr Slater's secretary comes into the office. "Alexa Hobermeyer wants to talk to you," she says.

"OK," says Mr Slater.

"And she wants to talk to Carrie and Alice too."

"We are all here," says Mr Slater. "Please ask Ms Hobermeyer to join us."

Alexa Hobermeyer comes into Mr Slater's office and sits down. She does not know anything about Saturday night. She wants to talk about her photo shoot.

"William!" she says to Mr Slater. "*Glitzy* magazine is a good client for your company. I want you to do something to help me!"

"Yes, Alexa," says Mr Slater. "What can I do to help you?"

"We are doing a special feature for next month's magazine about the modern West Coast Woman. On Saturday, I arranged a photo shoot for *Glitzy* magazine. It was very bad! The location was no good. It didn't look right. The model didn't have the right look. She couldn't ride a horse!

"The clothes are beautiful, and I borrowed some wonderful jewellery from Carrie. But I have to do the photo shoot again. I want Carrie to be the model."

Alexa looks at Carrie. "Can you ride a horse?"

"Yes," says Carrie. "I have two horses, but I can't be a model! I am not pretty! My nose is too big!"

Alexa laughs. "Anyone can be pretty," she says. "Real models have interesting faces. You will be perfect."

Alexa looks at Mr Slater. "William! I want you to give Carrie some time off work."

"Yes," says Mr Slater. "That will be OK, but I will have to find someone to do the accounts while she is away."

"No, I don't think so. Carrie will only be away for two or three days. I have to find a new location. I'm thinking about Oregon."

Carrie says, "My parents have a farm in Oregon. Maybe it would be a good place for your photo shoot."

"I'll look at it," says Alexa.

"And William," says Alexa. "I want you to find a new receptionist. I want Alice in my team. I saw her on Friday night. I saw the way she dressed Carrie. I like her style."

Alexa tells Carrie to call her father.

Carrie's father is very surprised, but he says it is OK if *Glitzy* want to do a photo shoot on the farm.

"I'll send some people up to Oregon to look at the farm," says Alexa. "They will take some photographs and send them to me.

"If I like it, we will do the photo shoot next Saturday. And, William, get a new receptionist today. I want Alice to start working in my team tomorrow."

12. SATURDAY

Alexa likes the farm. She thinks it will be a good place for the photo shoot. On Friday afternoon, Alexa's team goes to Portland. Alice and Carrie go with them. Alice has been working for Alexa for only three days, but she is very busy and happy.

They stay in an expensive hotel In Portland, and drive to Carrie's father's farm very early the next morning.

It is a very interesting day. Carrie changes clothes many times. The hairdresser changes Carrie's hairstyle many times. Carrie rides her horses. The photographers take hundreds of pictures.

Then everyone goes down to Ben's store. They take many pictures of Carrie.

Carrie's mother and father invite everyone to a BBQ on the farm.

Alexa comes to talk to Carrie. "The food is delicious!" she says. "And the photo shoot was a big success. I am very pleased.

"Your mother is very beautiful and very special. Will you help me talk to her?"

Carrie takes Alexa to talk to her mother. Alexa talks and Carries translates into sign language.

"Your jewellery is very beautiful. Everyone will want to buy 'Jewellery by Paulina'," says Alexa. "You will get a lot of money. I want to have an article about you, in the magazine. I want to have some photographs of you in the article. What do you think?"

---*It's OK. I'm pleased you like my necklaces, bracelets and earrings. But I don't want to leave the farm. This is my life. I could not be happy in a city.*---

Carrie explains her mother's thoughts to Alexa.

Alexa laughs. "It will make a very good story in *Glitzy*! And of course, your mother doesn't have to go anywhere. I will go and tell the photographers to come and take some pictures of your mother." She walks away.

---I wanted you to have adventures. But you did more than that. You brought adventure here to the farm. And I am pleased about the money. Your father will not have to work so hard. And I have a daughter who will be a famous model. --- Paulina is very happy.

---I don't want to be a famous model,--- Carrie signs back. *---Maybe I would like to do photo shoots sometimes. But I have my dream job, doing the accounts at the advertising agency.---*

---You must throw your work clothes in the garbage and buy some new clothes to wear to work!---

Carrie hugs her mother. *---OK! OK! OK!---*

THANK YOU

Thank you for reading Dressed for Success. (Word count: 6,381) We hope you enjoyed it.

There are quizzes about this book on our free study site I Talk You Talk Press EXTRA. http://italk-youtalk.com

If you would like to read more graded readers, please visit our website http://www.italkyoutalk.com

Other Level 2 graded readers include
Adventure in Rome
Andre's Dream
A Passion for Music
Christmas Tales
Danger in Seattle
Don't Come Back
Finders Keepers…
Hunted in Hong Kong
Marcy's Bakery
Men's Konkatsu Tales
Salaryman Secrets!
Stories for Halloween
The Cruise Ship
The House in the Forest
The Perfect Wedding
The School on Bolt Street

Train Travel
Trouble in Paris
Women's Konkatsu Tales

ABOUT THE AUTHOR

I Talk You Talk Press is an award-winning Japan-based publisher of language textbooks, graded readers and language learning/teaching resources.

Our team is made up of highly experienced language teachers and translators, who have all studied at least one additional language to an advanced level.

This experience enables us to design our materials from the perspective of both the teacher and the learner. We consult with both teachers and language learners when designing our textbooks and graded readers, and test our materials extensively in the classroom before publication.

We are a fast-growing press, and currently publish graded readers for learners of English. We publish new graded readers monthly.

www.ingramcontent.com/pod-product-compliance
Lightning Source LLC
Chambersburg PA
CBHW032005060426
42449CB00031B/805